Hark Valley

Sophia Campbell

WESTBOW
PRESS®
A DIVISION OF THOMAS NELSON
& ZONDERVAN

WestBow Press books may be ordered through booksellers or by contacting:

WestBow Press
A Division of Thomas Nelson & Zondervan
1663 Liberty Drive
Bloomington, IN 47403
www.westbowpress.com
1 (866) 928-1240

ISBN: 978-1-9736-8762-7 (sc)
ISBN: 978-1-9736-8763-4 (hc)
ISBN: 978-1-9736-8761-0 (e)

Library of Congress Control Number: 2020904762

Print information available on the last page.

WestBow Press rev. date: 5/4/2020

I dedicate this book to my wonderful family:
My daughters Farrah and Thalia, your contagious laughter and love drives
me wild. My wonderful husband for his consistent support and love.

Contents

My Songs of Victory for You

My Songs of Redemption for You

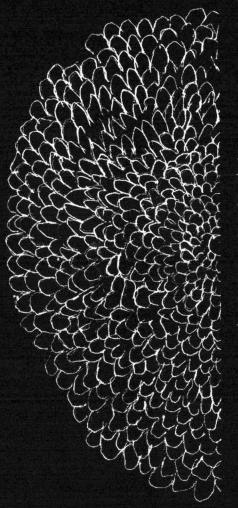

MY
SONG
OF
PRAISES
FOR
YOU

Your Amazing Love

⎯⎯⎯⎯✦⎯⎯⎯⎯

Many times I see
just how amazing your love is
for no matter how many times I fall, I stumble,
you are there, waiting to pick me up.

It is too much for me to fathom,
too great for me to comprehend;
my mind cannot contain this love,
yet you are there, waiting for me to visit with you.
Oh, my Lord, do you ever get overwhelmed with me,
my failures, my stumbles, my weaknesses?
How may I learn from you to pattern your ways
for repetitions and weaknesses are embedded in me?

My journey with you has become stagnant,
one more fall, one more stumble,
but with each, your arms get wider, longer, stronger.
They are filled with grace, mercy, and peace.

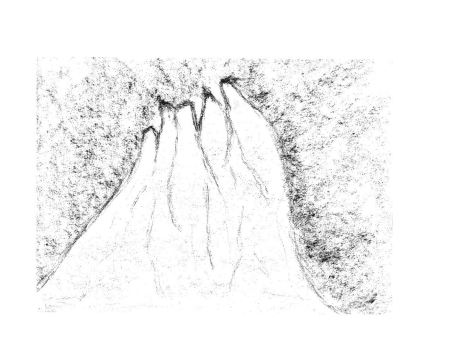

On the Pinnacle with You

Where can I go from your company,
your love, your protection, your grace?
If I go to the depths of the valleys or
the pinnacle of your mountains, even there you abide.

Many times my thoughts are about you.
I wonder what you think of me.

I feel far away from you;
it doesn't take too long for me to stumble.
I am a thousand miles from you,
yet my conscience clings to you.

Why do you pursue me
when hopelessness searches and seeks for me?
I lie on the hard ground before you,
spilling my heart before you.
Quietly you hear,
waiting for me to be as crystal before you.

I am overwhelmed; myriad emotions wash over me.
Grace welcomes me,
and you embrace me with mercies and grace.

In Wonder

—〰—

I often wonder about your love.
Why me, a sinner? Nothing special lies within me.

Then I am drawn to praise you. I contemplate you;
my very breath belongs to you.
All my days are in your hands, my paths already known.

You see through me as a clear reflection on still waters,
yet more like the hanging mirror.
I am like the blind lamb before you
yet an instrument of praise for you.

You have ordained work that you designed just for me
for you etched out my life
with the number of days allotted me.

I will surrender my heart, feet, and hands to you
for you have smiled on me with
showers of love and infinite mercies.

But I Murmur

Do you sometimes get tired of my whining, O Lord?
I specialize in this. I am weak; I scream!
What is my excuse?
Since you are strong,
why would you want any part of me?

There are no answers on the horizon.

Why should the eternal God of the heavens
even consider me?
The evil one begins his work; he schemes, lies, and captures.

I belong to a saving God, I declare!
I am not a part of your scheme.
Spread your wings elsewhere
for I have been redeemed, saved,
blessed, and highly favored
by the one who made the heavens and earth.

Such Privilege for Me

Wherever I am, you are there. What privilege for me.
I meet with you anywhere, anytime.
I can approach you with all things for
you are never overwhelmed by my presence.

With you, all my fears are at ease.
All my appointments with you
are unscheduled, unbiased, unintentional.
You are my rock.
All day long you are quietly waiting for me to visit
Why do you pour so much care and love on a mortal of my kind?

During my visits with you over the years
pitiful, I was blind to your light.
Now I am constantly at your feet,
like the weaning child with his mother,
but you never withdraw your portion of patience,
care, and unwavering love.

Your Hand in Mercy

For sure, time moves forward,
your love is constant,
and history is in the past;
everything revolves around time.

But you are constant, O Lord.
Your love, grace, and mercies are constant.

You see my humanness spilled out in rich, deep hues
for my sin parades itself before you.

I am in awe of your presence.
This moment I am grateful for grace
for it has favored me, granted me hope.

May I then bask in the mercies you bought for me.

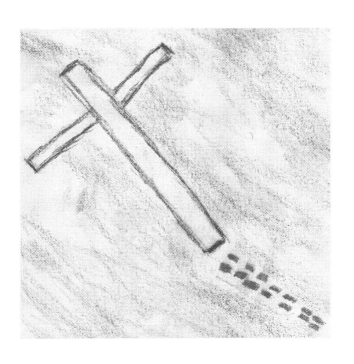

My Anchor

For with you all my days are constant;
my feet, they are anchored in you, my journey safe.

What privilege for me; a stalwart in freedom I am in you.
All day long, I am reminded of your presence.
Wherever I am, you are shielding me.

Your right hand is powerful,
your breath like a flaming sword.

The heavens cannot contain you,
yet you have hewed out a small space for you,
somewhere you know, a place in my heart and home.
There you visit.

Equality

―⁓―

All your children are equal before you, O Lord,
each one covered with your grace.
We all strive for an identity, for your love and mercies.

Our souls bought with your priceless blood.
Our hope is in you.

You bought us and redeemed us.
We are free in you.
Such privilege for me and your children!
For what can compare with your hope?

There is no need for strife among your children
for that is not our journey with you.
Our journey is built on your love and faith
for this is our journey with you.

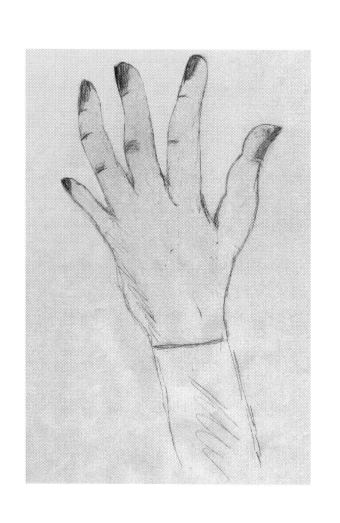

My Portion

—⟁—

All my days are measured out in your hands.
All I have acquired is what you have purposed for me.
I praise you with all my being.

From the increase of your hands,
I bring a spotless offering before you.

You know me by name; you carve out each smile on my lips.
I am bewildered at your works.

Your creation showers beauty round about me,
from lofty mountains to the dainty colored flower petals
etched with such intricate designs.

I am in awe of your vastness set before me.
Yet how gentle you are.

You have called out to me
and set me apart for your purposes.
I answer because I love you.

While I am vocal with my imperfections,
your steady hands are perfect for my incapability.

When I look at your creations, I am reminded
I am the clay, and you are the potter.

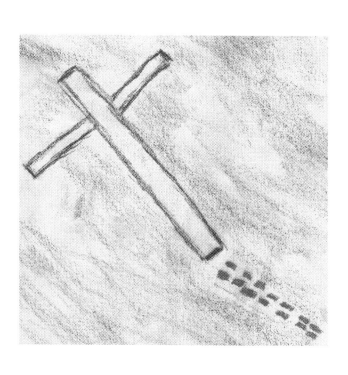

Your Constant Mercy

O Lord, you have been with me from days of old.
You have been my help from morning till dusk.
All day long you wait on me;
you ponder on things that are only for me.

You etch out my paths before you.
Unworthy as I am, I find myself at your feet.
Your mercies I seek.
I listen for your counsels
for I know they are pearls for my life.

Your presence embraces my being
Like a warm sheep blanket.
I fit perfectly in your hands.

I close my eyes; you are beside me.
Your thoughts are on me.

Your mighty right hand
is not short to deliver me from my fears,
and when I call upon your name,
you never grow weary of extending your help.

You never leave me
for you always abide with your maidservant.

My Questions

In the stillness of night, all I hear is your voice.
I feel deep sympathy and compassion for myself.
I am the sinner, lost, confused, and blind,
yet I have a yearning to work for you, to create for you.

When are you going to instruct my path?
How can my feet and hands serve you?

Then I hear your voice.
It is music to my troubled soul, how soothing.
When screams of a wailing child are on my lips,
your voice is hushed and calm.

You, O Lord, are majestic and powerful.
Your work is inspired all in a matter of your time.
I will spend my time with you
for here I find my complete joy.

Directed Path

O Lord, you were with me
from when I was in my mother's womb.
You saw me and chose me.
You see me as no one sees me.

I am known to you.
I am hand selected, picked out,
washed off, and laid out before you.
My thoughts and heart are but a mirror before you.
Like priceless gold.
I am more to you than gold.

You, O God, are like the oyster,
but I am like the dirt; you surround me.
I am the irritant speck in you.

For you made the pearl to shine brilliantly amid its dirt origins.
I remain priceless before all your works.
Nothing ever takes that away, nothing can compare.
I am priceless, unique before you.

My soul searches for you.
I will wander after you like a child
who is joyous before his parent.

I am moved by your love for me
for you made me and love me.

Fine Things

I must seek after your Word for time is measured.
Each day has afforded me new mercies and grace.

What do I do with this hope, this time?
It has become a luxury.

Do not allow me to get caught up, O Lord,
caught up with self.

Allow your maidservant
my portion of your counsels and truth,
Your truth that shines forth from your Word.

Brush me off, O Lord.
Polish my heart, my tongue, and my hands
for your time is grace to me.
Then will I stand with you.

This time you have allowed me
is a treasure and a gem.
It can never be reclaimed,
so allow your servant to be still and listen for you
that I may thrive before you
like the much-watered olive tree.

The Truth, the Way

—✕✕—

Many times I fall before you, O Lord.
Many times I falter and fail,
but you call me by name.

You place me where I am today;
you know my circumstance.
You know all about me, O Lord,
you care deeply about me.
You have a plan for my life,
and you instruct my heart and path.

There is nothing that you will not deliver me from
for you have given me victory already.

Remove the veil from my eyes.
Allow me to see you,
O Lord, in all your glory and majestic splendor.
For surely you are the way the truth and light.

I Wobble

I ask that you may lighten my load
to make my pathway easier.
Create a cushion for my calloused hands and feet;
Oh, my Lord, they have become sore and rough.

You have sustained and rescued me.
You help me carry my load and burdens.

Like the jaguar that rushes for his prey,
so are you quick to rescue and save me.
I thank you for all you have done.

I will continue to pour out my praises upon you,
to serve you, though undone I may be.

With all that you have afforded me,
I will honor your name, praising you continuously
until I become faint and weary before you, O Lord.

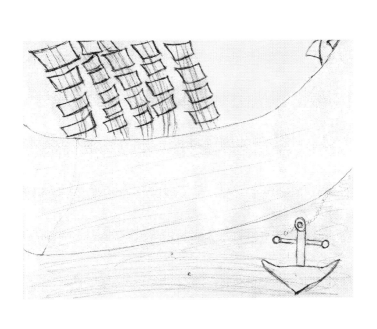

The Heavy Cargo Ship

—◦◦◦—

I am waiting on you, O Lord.
I sit quiet and still.
My mind filled with questions,
my feet anchored with troubles, like heavy brass,
my tears running all day like the swelling river.

But I am like a jagged cliff with highs and lows.
I am etched with doubts that plant themselves in my heart.
I am being swallowed up in doubts daily.

Surely I am not equipped with your light, your truth.
Such sadness for me,
my mind frail and unable to understand your Word.

I am content with being quiet before you
for I have traveled this path before.
But today you will prepare my heart
for a feast in your Word.

Surely you will make your
maidservant understand your truth,
bring light to your Word,
for only then will my soul be anchored fully in you.

What Mighty Power

—◆◆◆—

O Lord, my God, you are awesome and amazing,
from the gentle bleating of lambs you hear
to the mighty swaying of cedar trees.

You are from everlasting to everlasting;
you are beautiful and majestic.
Even towering mountains parade themselves before you
and the soaring eagles you take note of.

How could I not serve a God like you?
How could I not offer my praises?
For surely my voice will trumpet
praises before you, all my praises for you.

With you all things are sure, are possible,
for my pinnacle of troubles humbles itself before you.

Do not be far away from me, O Lord.
For I will be desperate before you.
I will lie lonely, helpless without you.

Fill me, O Lord, with your sweet fragrance
that I may be shielded from the tempter's doubt.
Preserve my spirit that I maybe armored in your strength.

Your Hands

O Lord, how powerful and awesome you are.
Your mighty hand
is never short in answering my prayers.

When your children cry out to you
from gutters of deep despair, you will hear and deliver us.
You will stretch forth your hands from on high
in your dwelling place to remove everything that stifles us.
You rescue us over and over again from calamities.

You command the storms
and winds to change their courses.

Who else has the power that you command?
Indeed, you are mighty and amazing.
I will continue to serve you all the days of my life
with all your strength that you have afforded me.

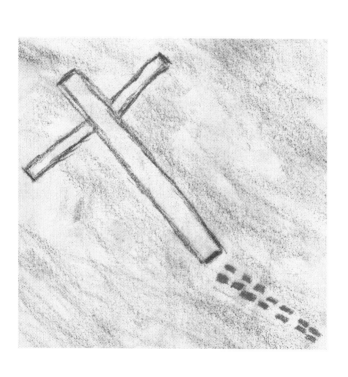

Your Power

———◆———

Show me your purposes, O Lord,
that I may build my house upon
that one you have selected for me,
so your glory can shine forth like the streaming sunlight.

You saw me from my mother's womb.
A special name you have picked for me.
You show me your paths.

Your grace and mercies are like beads of pearls
about my neck for with each pearl there is no ending.

My entire existence is because of you.
I throw myself at your feet
for there is no other place I would choose.

But I am like the wanderer before you,
searching for your guidance and counsel
from everything else but you.

Make haste to answer me, O Lord.
Do not keep silent around me.
Do not keep silent around me.

Take me to the treasury
of your counsel and understanding.
Allow me your measure of wisdom
that I may be filled, yet not puffed up.

Grant me according to your allotment to do your will.
Allow me to serve you, O Lord,
that hopelessness may not abound.

Allow me the status of servanthood
for that is the highest calling in my life.

Summer

Just now as I glance out, it is sunny with a steady breeze.
The tops of the pine sway gently;
the grass lies mellow in the soft wind.

Now I am happy; I feel so happy.
I wish I could take my piece of happiness
and share it with others, those who struggle to smile.
What peace, what joy, pure joy.

Happiness, like little presents, are given to us.
In nature, your stamp of beauty is marked
with majestic brilliance.

Your mountaintops are soothing to my eyes.
Sheer joy echoes deep within me
as I stroll through the green grass,
such soft luxury.
In the morning, as I glanced out,
I beheld your creation
so vast my mind drowns in pure awe.

The towering trees, your shiny silvery clouds
cast their spells of beauty and majesty round about me.
I am wrapped tightly in the blanket of your warm sunlight.
Such beauty, such privilege for me.

A New Year

My heavenly Father,
how it pains me when I feel so broken
when I am miles away from you.

Yet it is not quite that way; you are always near.
Even my thoughts are like crystal before you
for I am your child.

As the new year dawns,
be near to me, O Lord, be near.
I contemplate in silence before you.
I wait for you, your counsel, guidance, your help.

O Lord, preserve my soul.
It is you that I wait on, no one else.
I know you are near me.
I know you have heard my cries.
I will remain in you for you are right beside me.

I Boast in You

And what of me, Holy Father,
that you are mindful of me?

You know me; you know my days.
My breath is measured out before you.
My thoughts, my desires, and my intentions
are clear before you, as clear as dawn.

Your plans for me
are like crowns of jewels upon my head.
They prolong my days.

Though I gamble with your time,
I waste away in indecisiveness,
you know my destiny.
You take pity on me and grant me hope and a purpose.

Fill me with your purposes, O Lord, my God.
Consider this maidservant as your helper.
Fill me with your passions, your works, your thoughts.

Polish me that I may shine
for even the dazzling diamond cannot compare.
So I would rejoice and testify of your goodness to me;
I choose to magnify you
for you made me to speak, grow, and boast in you.

I Am Made Complete in You

How do I fit in the palm of your creations, O God?
Why should you consider me?

I weep because of your pure love for me.
Love that is tested in the fire
flows to all your children; it brings me to my knees.

But for me, I am found with much instability.
I am decorated beautifully with impatience.
Yet you consider one such as me.

My heart, my purposes, will you seal it, O Lord,
seal in rich colors of your mercies and love?

For surely my voice would be raised for you;
my hands would clap with rich melodies for you.
And when my heart surrenders,
may it be only for your purposes and will.

Be hasty to be with your daughter, your maidservant,
and make me complete in you.

You Remind Me Who You Are

—⁓—

O Lord, I am but a speck before you.
What do you see in me?
Is the answer hidden far away from me?

Yet you see a soul, one that can sing before you,
made to praise and worship you,
a soul you have redeemed, a soul bought,
so redemption shines majestically for you.

O Father,
remind me of your blood.
Remind me of your sacrifice.
Remind me, O Lord, of your grace.

I Am Laden with Your Blessings

O Lord, you have afforded your daughter
and her household such luxuries, such peace, such blessings.

What have I done to be so favored in your sight
that you should be mindful of even me?
Am I called out differently from your children, O Lord?

All my days and time are indebted to you.
Every fiber of my being is indebted to you.
I will praise you; I will pour out my heart to you.

Surely I will give you all my strength,
my honor, my allegiance.

Even though I may walk,
it is not me, but you, O Lord,
you who sustains me, strengthens me,
and causes my heart to be laden with your joy.

Your Mighty Hands

Oh, my Father, why should you consider even me?
Why should you attend to every detail of my woes?
You even honor every one of my pleas.
O Lord, you are mindful of me.

For I am just a speck before you,
yet I will serve you, my household,
and all you have given to me.
I will not cease from serving you.
How can I continue my walk without you?
How can I raise up my household without you?
A tabernacle without you?

O Lord, I continue my journey in you,
so my days are extended.
I will persevere in you.
I will bow my knees before you.
I will be sustained in you.

My Pure Joys in You

Should faith have its voice, what sound would it be?
Would God hear?

Yet he knows us by the quantity of faith we have;
too little, he is sad, and with much,
it would be well for my soul.

He knows how we were made; he knows our frame.
As for me, O Lord, when trials pursue me,
they become stumbling blocks before me.
Allow my faith to grow, to thrive before you.

I come before you with all you have given me,
all your strength, mercies, and love.
May you lift me up to a higher place
where you are found.

A Higher Place

—⁓—

Count me, O Lord, as your child. Like a mother who glances
on her bunch and knows I am her gem.
So am I with you, O Lord, the crown jewel of all your creations.

Allow me the status to shine for you,
to stand tall for you, to work for you
so my days will not be filled with hopelessness, emptiness,
busy chasing after the beautiful butterfly
that soon goes its own way.

For your ways are filled with victory for me;
your work, your purposes, your mighty hand will sustain me.
They will preserve me so my days will be extended for
your services.

No Limits

I could scatter volumes of my pride,
yet still have enough for thousands to spare.

I could scatter volumes of my impatience,
yet still have enough for hundreds to share.
I could scatter volumes of my arrogance,
yet still have enough for thousands to use.

Why should you even consider me, O Lord?
Why should you even tarry with me?

I am so bewildered by your love
that you would even consider me.
Yet you do.

You have hewn out a place for me at Calvary.
You have made me to sit among those who call upon your name.

Your blood has no price, no limits,
yet it was bought for me.

Such provisions make me dazed.
Your love stifles every human part in me.
I am in complete awe of you.

Hold My Hands

Hold my hand, O Lord,
lest I lose my way.

I will follow you for you made me,
and you know just what my needs are.
I am protected and loved by you.

You are majestic, powerful, and loving.
There is nothing that compares to you.
There is no one whom I esteem before you.
You are my anchor.
You have become my shelter, my abode.

How marvelous you are,
how majestic, how beautiful.

How loving you are, O God,
that you tarry patiently with me.

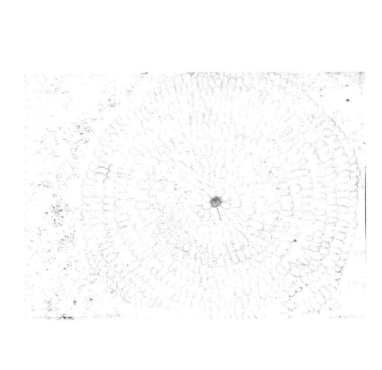

I Am in Awe of You

—◦◦◦—

O Lord, make your directions and paths
clear to your maidservant.
Decorate the walls of my home with your guidance.
Fill my home with your presence.

In far distances, the hills are outlined
clearly and beautifully before me;
they are set in pure grandeur.
So are your handiworks before me;
they glisten with such splendor.

You, O God, shall direct me to your paths.
You shall outline your paths brightly before me.
There is nothing hidden from your children
when our hearts cling to
and our faith is carved out for you.
You

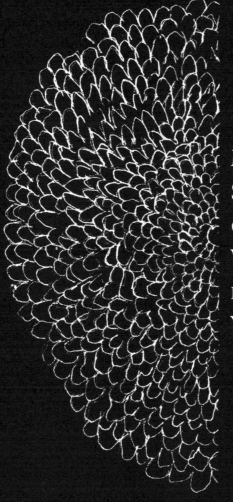

My
Songs
of
Victory
for
You

At Your Feet

There are fragments in me, O Lord,
pieces of my heart decorated heavily
with doubts, and I feel I am undone,
unworthy before you.

My shortcomings, my insecurities, doubts, and fears
are like huge rocks; they separate me from you.
Such sadness for me.

Yet you have made provisions for all my shortcomings.
Your blood washes over me, washes every stain,
and I am made clean again, whole.

How much love you pour on me.
Your provisions are too much for me to fathom.
There are no words that can describe this love.

No artist can capture this scene on paper.
I am bewildered by you.

Then let me bask in the love you have laid up for me.
Let me bathe in the freedom you provide
for I am considered to be among
those who sit at your feet.

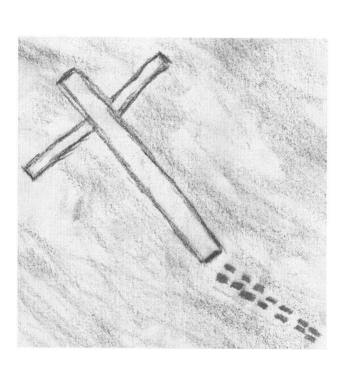

Directing My Path

—◆—

O Lord, keep my eyes on you
for both my inner and outer voices
are stained with humanity.

O Lord, keep my eyes focused on you
for my words are tainted with contention.
I have the capacity to sink to a low place
where you are not present, and my voice beckons mercy before you.
Shield me, O God,
and preserve my soul from the pangs of sin,
where my mind is consumed with self.

My hands and eyes have become soaked in vanity
for with self, the windows of heaven are closed.

Make haste, O Lord,
to snatch me from the one who lurks
and trembles in your presence.
Do not allow your maidservant to tread upon his ground
for with him calamities rage,
confusion and despair shake hands with him as friends,
pain and grief are hidden under the veil of deception.

Separate me, O God, from this deceiver.
Keep me from his home and kingdom.

The Scale

Place in the balances the weight of sin.
How much does anger weigh? Where is its comparison?
What can compare with malice?
If anger should spill on the ground, of what form would it be?

To whom do they belong?
Where are their owners? Their designers?
I do not wish to have any part with them.
For surely they are all weightless,
placed on the foundation of sound wisdom
and understandings from God.
For surely anger and malice will crumble, dissipate, be gone.

Guide me with your love, patience, hope, and mercy,
O God of the heavens and earth.
For where now lies anger, malice, and their counterparts?
They are dispersed, gone.
Just like their designer; soon he shall know his fate.

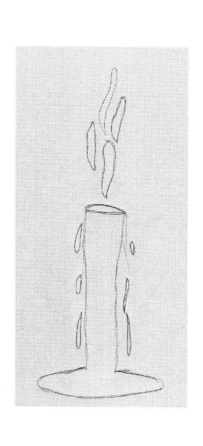

A Stormy Night

———

You redeemed and bought me; I am free in you.
This provision is too much for me to comprehend.
My capacity to understand your works is limited.
Your love is like a candle struck before me
during a stormy winter night.

The winds howl, the trees bend,
but the candle stands undaunted; its wick is full of oil.
So you are with your children;
your love stands undaunted.

In the midst of our sins, your mercies waiver not
for you redeem me. You love me, and I remain your child.

The Peasant

—⦿—

O Lord and Master, you weep day and night upon me,
over me, and with me. I am deeply loved by you.
Your love for me puts my mind in a trance; why me?

For I am a peasant and a sinner before you.
Your love pours out upon me, anoints my soul, head, feet.

I am desolate before you. I am pitiful, poised for disaster.
I am a breeding ground for instability.

But when I encounter my Creator,
you turn my mourning into a plan for you.
You establish my feet for your purposes.
You anchor me within you; I cannot be moved.

I have become like the chief merchant; about me lies purple,
and my household is nestled in your comforts.
Your words are a polished sword
for those who contend against me.
Your right hand guards my ways.

My hands, my heart are waxed shine for your bidding.
My days, they are laden with your purposes.

For how can I not serve a God like you
When surely you have pardoned me
for you make me to sit at your feet?

Your Shield

I am being led to the gutter constantly.
I am blind and unaware of my surroundings.
I am like the sheep being led to the slaughter.

Then I call upon your name out of despair,
and you answer me.
You rescue me all over again—
yesterday, today, tomorrow, constantly, consistently.
You sympathize and draw near to me.
Your love and care are from the beginning;
they never change.

How vast you are.
You are unknowing and unpredictable to us.
I cannot fathom your portion of love and care for me.
Like the universe, your love has no end.

Draw near to me, O Lord.

I hide in you, and you cover me day and night.
You shelter me
from those who want to destroy and steal,
from those who want to strengthen the kingdom of lies.

Therefore, my heart is hewn out just for you
So that I remain buoyed up in you.

A Secret Place

No one sees me as you do.
My eyes are hidden under a smile,
a smile known to you.

I am with you constantly,
a place where all my joys are found,
a place where my smile transforms.

There is no place here for anger,
just joy, peace, and happiness
brightly shone as the light of dawn.

I draw friends to you.
We meet in you.
We dine with you; we sing with you.
We pray with you; we unite in you
till we all surrender in you.

A Haughty Ride

In my heart, I ride on a chariot before you.
My prayers are placed in a golden box,
my thoughts and intentions plastered with goodness.
I am perfect before you for I take the time to seek you daily.

O Lord, many others don't know you;
they have no intentions to seek you or visit with you.
They busy themselves for their own benefits and successes.

Oh, chasten me, Lord, from my own thoughts
for I seek to find your goodness with my limited understanding.

I have built a moat around me;
it is filled with selfish praises.

I am engulfed in my own goodness and excellence.
I have raised myself to the pedestal of your excellence.

But all your children's intentions are known to you.
You know what is on our hearts; you search the heart.

So chasten me, O Lord; remind me who I am,
just a speck before you
in need of your never-ending mercies and grace.

Not Leaving

O Lord, do not let anything take away
my joy, which comes only from you.
Whatever it may be that determines to do so is
cunningly crafted by the evil one.

My joy is yours; my hope and future are in you.
In you, my foundations are laid out.
Keep me, O Lord, for I get overwhelmed
if I go far from your presence.

The Trap

A trap is laid out for me each day.
Its designer is a liar;
he devises and searches for flaws,
weaknesses, opportunities.

O Lord, cover me, and shield me under your care.
For if I stray, I am overwhelmed.

My weaknesses and insecurities seek me out.
Hide me, O Lord.
Equip me with a brass plate of your strength.

Cover me with your shield of mercy and grace,
and then put a new song on my lips.
For you will determine how far away
I am ever to go from you.

The Pearl

O Lord, you are with me from old.
You saw me and chose me.
You see me as no one else does; I am known to you.

I am hand-selected, picked out,
washed off, and laid out before you.
You see me as no one else sees me.

My thoughts and heart are discreet
and special before you.

My soul searches for you.
I will wander after you like a child after his parent.

I am moved by your love;
special and unique I am.

Lingering in You

—◦∿∿◦—

It is sad when I have to go far from your presence
for wherever I turn, I am embraced by my weaknesses.
But when I am in your presence,
strength and grace hold hands with me.

Oh, let me not go from you.
My joys are a crown I wear before you.
I am destined to be with you all day long.

My unknown future questions,
they hang about my neck like heavy metals dangling idly.
I am not equipped with your answers.

Surely sorrows and troubles are abundant,
and I am not equipped with your light.
Let me not go from your presence.
Allow me to linger where you abide,
so I may feed my hungry soul.
Hold on to me, that I may not go from your presence.
Your strength, peace, and counsel I hoard
for these have become like precious oil on my head.
I bathe in them.

Oh, let me not leave your presence;
let me stay just a bit longer.
My heart washes over with joy in your presence.
Allow me to linger before you.

The Future

There are times I wonder, *What does life mean?*
What is next? I anticipate good faith.
What is my role, my purpose?

Dear God,
What do you think of me?
What are your plans for me?
What lies ahead on the pathway?
Am I where you want me to be?

Instruct me, O Lord.
My destiny is with you, mighty God.
My pathway is determined by you.
You put my feet in a strong place.
You establish your precepts within me.

I am your child; my days are measured and accounted for in you.

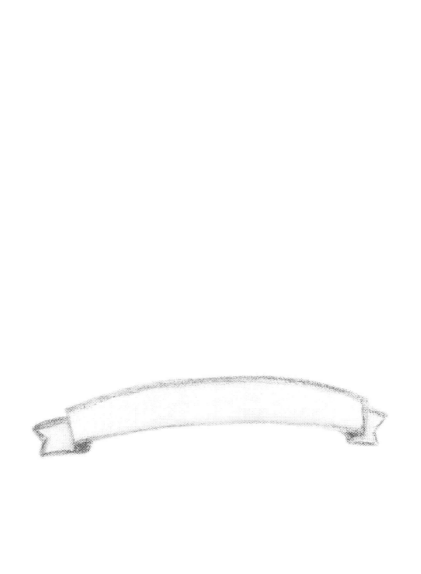

What Do I Wave?

What can I put before you, O Lord?
The God of this universe,
what do I wave before you as a banner?

Is it doubt, fear, stress?
Who made the heavens and seas?

Who rolled back the seas so Israel could walk?
Who fights for you?
Who mediates on your behalf?

I wrote this for you, Lord.
Let me shout praises to you, O God.
Everything is in God's time.

Taking the Reins

—⟡—

O Lord, my God,
many times I try to take the reins in my own hands.
I try to help you out.

It has become so easy to step before you.
It seems like eternity to hear your voice,
your words, your guidance.

But you are never too far away, O Lord.

You are always with me, guiding me
with outstretched arms,
unending love, and your mountains of grace.

Pardon my selfish heart; grant me overflowing mercies.
Then teach me to walk
in the steps you have laid right before me.

Hasten me to your Word that offers light and truth.

Then on my knees,
I will see your path before me.
I will run to you and hold on to you
Like the anchored ship on rough waters.

A Maze

Arguments, fights, contentions, and quarrels
are a maze before God's people,
designed as distraction to take away
and separate us from our God.

Glory and praises that should be given to God have fled;
our glory now shines for the deceiver.

Have mercy, O Lord, for the devil is crafty and zealous.
His intentions, he stores up and
then scatters wildly on God's people.

Make haste, O Lord, to put your seal around me.
Seal my heart on your purposes with your love,
so your glory will be lifted high with praises.

Cover and hide me under your wings.
May you strengthen your maidservant that I may run to you.

Your Comforting Presence

You are my guide, O Lord, my navigator.
I will never be lost with you.

Will you drive me, O Lord?
Let us go somewhere far away.
In any case, you started this journey with me;
you will surely finish it.

I trust you to do the driving.
I can fall asleep.
I will let my hair blow in the soft wind.

We don't need a GPS.
I won't be concerned with where we will go,
on the gas bill, or even what we will do
for you are majestic, powerful, caring, and all-knowing.

What fears would I have?

Would we make casual stops and go sightseeing?
Are we going straight to a destination?

What plans do you have for me?
Lead me, O Lord, for I am your passenger.

I Thrive in You

You made me to praise you,
to sing praises before you continually.
I am your master craft, a gem before you;
I am beautiful before you.

You were nailed on the cross for me.
You died for me.
Your whole life is a sacrifice for me.
You taught me how to pray, to love, to share;
my whole life will be a sacrifice before you.

I will choose to forgo what seems beautiful,
peaceful, and secure to your children.
But to you, it is a trap laden
with disasters and calamities for us.

The trap our world has placed its stamp of success on.

But as for me, I choose you,
your sacrifice, and your ways
for they are light and easy.

Your ways are designed just for me to thrive
and to be completely secure in you.
What marvelous hope for me.

A Tipping Point

O Lord, my biases and issues are known to you—
my strains, my sins, my prejudices, my limitations,
my inconsistencies, my weaknesses.
They are all known to you,
yet you embrace me amid these.

But why, O Lord?

Teach me your statutes, Lord,
for my prejudices are real, not imagined.
They are carved into my being;
they define me.

But you, O Lord, are willing to overlook
because you see who I am and who I can become.
Then extend your mercies to me, O Lord.
My voice cries deep within.

My brokenness and my humanness,
you took them all away.

You conquered all my iniquities,
and you won the battle of sin.
Teach me, O Lord, your Word and your truth
that I may not stray from you.

Persevering in You

God is in the business of saving lives.
He wishes no one to be lost, but
all to be saved and come into a saving relationship with him.

His business of saving his children from sin is steadfast.
His mercies for us thrive greatly in the face of adversities.

His mercy and grace gush over our
difficulties like mighty waves.

What of my role, my walk, and my purposes in you, O God?
It is already determined clearly before him
for God is amazing and all powerful.

His purposes for his children are vast.

Your Stronghold

How can your children thrive before you, O Lord?
You accept us just as we are.
Spotted and scared with sin,
yet you hold on to us like the mighty warrior,
never letting us go from you, such might and love.

Allow us not to wander in places of desolation,
places that seem like oases to us,
yet are dusty, dry deserts for you
where nothing thrives,
like stagnant water in the gutter.

Remember that we are frail.
Remember we are mortals before you;
we are blind, desolate, desperate,
and easily stray from you.

Preserve me, O Lord.
Preserve my spirit that I may remain close to you.
Keep me in your stronghold.

I will kneel before you and draw close to you
for you comfort me with your breath.

You Reign

—◦∿◦—

Can I count my days as dust? What authority do I have?
My questions stream themselves into my mind,
yet I choose not to answer.

I am not equipped with your truth.
You, who put breath in my nostrils,
I am accountable to you for all my days.

It is well for me to embrace hope.
My soul acknowledges you;
you are my God, a King, a Conqueror.

All that I have amassed is the portion you have allowed me.

I smile, live, and sing because of you.
Grant me the opportunity to be in your presence
for surely your beauty and majesty encompass where you are.

Yet there is another who canvasses for my joy, my soul.
He will surely flee from your presence
for the home of deception calls for him.

My joy, my praises, they belong only to you.
Stand up, O Lord,
remind me of his destiny.
Surely your truth and righteousness reign in all the earth.

Broken for You

—◦∿◦—

Bring me, O Lord, to your dwelling place.
Show me your paths and direction for my life.
Grant me your counsel;
instruct my hands, feet, and heart for your work.

Be near to me,
O God. Answer me when I cry out to you
for the breath I have is allotted.

Do not let me be puffed up with vain thoughts,
like the prideful peacock.

Answer me when I seek for you like buried treasure.
From dusk till morning, you have granted me strength.
Do not let me be like the wanderer,
with instabilities and no purposes.

Allow me to get caught in the thicket of your purposes.
Busy my thoughts toward you.
Channel my energies, oh, my Lord, only for you.
Then I may say my God has journeyed along with me.

I Am Your Servant

Have mercy on me, O God.
My voice you hear.
My faith calls to you; this is my sure pathway to you.

Like the roaring of jet engines,
the gears in right places, so is my faith in you.

I will soar to a higher place in you, new heights,
a place where my faith has been anchored in you.

You will guide me for your journey.

Though my path is already known to you,
you wait for me that I may join you to greater heights.
Anchor me in your faith as I soar.

Busy my hands and heart for your cause;
wrap me around your purposes, your will.

Blot out distractions and idleness.
These belong to the devil, his crowns.

Put a veil over my eyes when he is close
for his intentions are to snatch me away from our journeys.
Fashion my heart, O God.
Fashion my heart according to your will.

Put me in the center of your sphere.
Here dwells your missions, purposes, and will
so your work will be done.

Nestle me in your purposes and your plans, O Lord.

Though I am of little stature before you,
you consider me.
You name me, and then you consider me
among those who sit at your feet.

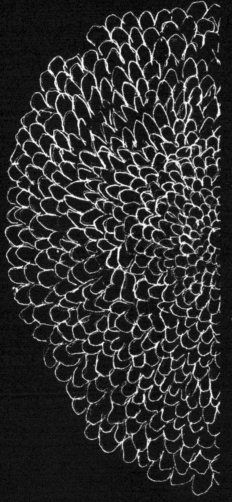

My
Songs
of
Redemption
for
You

Open Vessel

O Lord, my heart is like an open bottle before you.
Waiting to be filled, I stand and wait before you.

Teach me your words that I may speak.
Instruct me in your ways that I may act.
Show me your purposes that I may walk with you.

Oh, guide your daughter
for I am desperate to hear from you.
My heart searches only for you.

Remember that I am feeble. Lay your words in my heart.
Be near to me, O Lord,
for I remain your servant.

I Will Not Leave Your Presence

O Lord, I am penitent before you.
I seek after your counsel and guidance.

I will not leave till you have vindicated me,
till you have overshadowed me
with your grace and mercies.

I know you are near. You hear my voice,
but you already know my thoughts.
You know my petitions.

You were nailed to the cross for me
till you won and have conquered.

Such love and mercy you pour upon me
your vast oceans cannot contain them.

Such powerful hope and marvelous grace you left for us
in this chaotic world.
It has become our treasures, our legacies.

Like the mirror that does not deceive,
so I reflect your love and patience through my intentions.
You have made provisions for my shortcomings
for you see how feeble I am.

O Lord, let me not leave from your presence.

You Teach Me to Walk

Teach me to walk, O Lord.
Even though I am grown,
I stumble and wobble before you.

You are not amused or entertained.
You are more concerned with how often I rise,
how much I can persevere in you.

You invite me to hold your hand
for you already know how weak I am.
Surely you will strengthen me.

You know my full intentions and my burden limits.

Such love, patience, and care you pour upon me,
it floods my soul.
For even the magnitudes of your raging seas,
your vast oceans, pale in comparison to the
depth your love has for me.

Yet without anger, disappointment, mockery,
even impatience, you allow me to choose freely
your love or my own strength.
I choose your hand, O Lord, your strength and your paths.

You Who Rescues

—✦—

Many times I fall before you.
I fall deeper and deeper into sin; I feel far away from you.

Sadness envelops my being like a warm blanket,
such warmth, comfort. I snuggle in despair.
Sadness speaks to me, and I am alone, desolate.

I listen for you.
I come slowly before you on my knees.
It doesn't matter where I may be.
I pour my soul before you.

Then grace encompasses me,
reminding me of the victory I have in you.
Grace and mercy, they pour themselves upon me.
Like the cascading waterfall gushing over the rocks,
they pin me to the ground.

I cannot escape this love.
I am overshadowed, captivated.
Stifled by its power, it soothes my soul.

Your love has rescued me once twice, thrice …
For who can count the sum of it all?
Now I take delight in my deliverance in you;
such comfort, hope, and such love you give.

My Visit with You

I enjoy our times together,
long moments on my knees before you.
I cry, and you hold me.

You remind me that you won the battle already.
I lie on my bed now,
sick, too weak to walk, sore.

Emptiness and desolation, they are right beside me.
I am engulfed in a pool of despair.

Then I see you again, on the cross this time,
bloodied, with a sorrowful crown on your head,
a sword pierced in your side.

It is then that I'm reminded of your victory for me.
A surge of hope and victory rushes through my veins.
They captivate me; I am drenched with your love.
I rejoice; laughter gushes fourth like mighty waves on my lips.
Oh yes, sweet victory you won already on the cross.

In my weakest moments,
I am reminded of your victory for me.
For while you were nailed to the cross, broken,
your victory shone in majestic splendor
just for me.
Such a feast for my troubled mind.

My Imperfections

All my days are in your hands.
All I have is what you have purposed for me.
I praise you with all my being.
I bring an offering before you.

You know me.
You carve out each smile on my lips.
I stand bewildered at your works.
Your works speak to me.

I am fearful of your vastness before me,
yet how gentle are your ways.

You call me, and then you wait.
Not imposing. No indulgence.
I return your call because I love you.

Your steady hand is perfect for my incapability.
I have become like the broken record
with my imperfections before you.

Then you show me your works.
I am then reminded
surely I am the clay, and you are the potter.

You Are for Me

———·∾∾·———

You are for me; you are with me.
You are not against me.
All your provisions are for me.
Therefore, I thrive before you.

You rescue me and hear me when I cry.
You rescue me with your mighty right hand.

My paths are like thickened tar before me.
I feel overwhelmed and burdened.
I have become blind, and gloom embraces me.

Yet my thoughts and heart are clear before you.
Your mercies, oh, your compassion toward me!
Your love for me stifles my capacities to worry.

But when you see me, you see your Son's blood.
It is then you call me by name.

Do Not Be Far from Me

Do not be far from me, O Lord,
for trouble is not far away.
He seeks for me and tries to destroy and break me.

But you see my path before you.
Your path for me is already etched out.
Troubles come; they go.
Where it leaves me has become desperate and foolish.
I will arise and run to you
for if I remain, I will be beaten and battered once, twice, thrice.
I will become like the dried stick,
easily broken and withered.

Victory calls for me and raises its voice.
It is loud and audible for me.
I will run to you for you will rescue and deliver me.

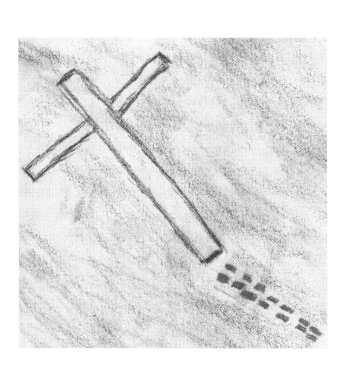

Your Amazing Love

My almighty Father, in you I put my trust.
My entire being searches for you and seeks you out.
In you I find great comfort and peace.
I long to hear from you.

You are awesome and amazing
for all blessings come from you.

You clothe your children in strength through your Word.
Your mercy, grace, and hope fill us with comfort.
We are anchored in you;
nothing can separate us from your love.

You rule the heavens and earth
from everlasting to everlasting.
Such great hope for me, for your children
in this darkened world.

Chasing after Me

⸻

O Lord, strife, anger, and doubt seek me.
They search for me all day long.
They constantly seek an audience with me.

But seal me, O Lord,
put your flaming sword around me
with your Word and your light.

Do not allow your maidservant
to stumble before you;
your mighty right hand is never too short to save me.

Deliver and make haste to rescue me
for I become weary from fighting.
Anger and doubts invade my mind like angry waves,
constantly, consistently the ebb and flow in my heart.

The evil one has no good intentions for me.
But it is you, O Lord, that I seek after.
My soul finds comfort and strength in you.

Do not leave me, O Lord.
Make accommodation for your maidservant
at your altar, so there I may dwell.
There I find complete hope.

My Journey with You

You fight all my battles, O Lord.
Pave the way for me to thrive before you.
Answer when I call out to you.
Provide for my household needs.
Surely you are with me.

But what of my journey with you?
All my needs are provided for.
My praises are on my lips to you.
To you I give my honor.
I worship you with every breath you have given me.
Surely you are God Almighty.

My journey begins with you.
My paths have become clear before me
for you provide your understanding
and guidance to me.
So then may I worship you all my days.

You Found Me

—∿—

O Lord, my God, I am scared,
too scared to go forward.
I cannot hear you; I cannot see you.
My faith is tested; I am heading to a dark place.

Like water flowing in the desert,
so my hope remains futile.
I make myself small and fit in a tiny place.
I shrink and get in a small place where it is warm and cozy.

But you, O Lord, want to rescue and deliver me.
You want to remind me
of days that you have delivered me.
You want to make my fears and doubts
stop having their tight grip on me,
so I may be free in your love and thrive before you.

You knock on my heart,
but my thoughts are too negative.
They drown you out.

My mind is busy with worries.
A veil covers my thoughts.
I separate myself from you; I have become dormant.
I remain distant from you.

Then you remind me through your Son's blood,
your hope and love are poured upon me.

My thoughts ease from the hold of fears.
I can hear the sounds of victory.
Victory screams to me;
my whole body shivers from your joy.

I stand tall and run to you like the lost child
who sees his parent close by.

You Rescue Me

As I walked through the park sore, tired, and lame,
I asked God where he was in my life.
He turned my head westward to heaven
to show me his glory.

"This is the heavens," he declares, "not man-made,
and creation not man-made. There I dwell among them."
As I drove home broken, penniless, sore, sick, tired,
I asked God where he was and what I should do.

I was reminded of Elijah and all the false prophets,
the great victory for Elijah.
I rejoiced mightily;
a melodious song rang through my heart.

I know God is the same yesterday, today, and tomorrow.
He will surely rescue me.

I Wait on You

I am waiting on you, O Lord.
I sit quiet and still,
my mind is filled with questions.

I'm not anchored in my walk with you.
I want to, but I am so desperate
for my faith runs dry like the dry, dusty road.

I seem to drift even further away from you.

I am content with sitting quietly before you,
though it seems everlasting.
I have traveled this path before;
I am laden with its experience.

But today, you will help me to start a new journey.

A Mighty God

———✦———

O Lord, my God, you are so awesome and amazing.
You are from everlasting to everlasting.

You are the God that is in the saving business
for on your holy hours, you mend my brokenness.

You provide windows of opportunity
for grace and mercy to flow through me.

I rejoice and take delight in you.
For over and over again I witness
your mighty right hand before me.

Oh, that you would have compassion on me,
your maidservant.

You are my rock, my shield,
a mighty warrior
for you quench all the fiery flames about me.

It may seem that all my surroundings
have become like stagnant waters,
nothing moves, no signs of life around.
Yet you are already opening
doors and opportunities that I may thrive for you.

The Gift of Life

Life is a gift I get to bask and thrive in.
Though catastrophes, wars, and pestilence rage,
I am covered with your presence.

You put your hedge around me,
and my foot is anchored in you.
O kind Jehovah, how beautiful you are.
My days unfold like the budding rose before you,
and I await your calm, soothing words.
They echo in my ears; they heal my bruised mind.

All around me illuminate for your light is brighter
than ten thousand of your angels.
Who can hide from your beam?

Your children wait penitently for your touch.
Remind us, O Father, of our feeble frames.
Our days, our time, our strengths, and freedom are all a loan.
It is borrowed time that seeks for your instruction
and maps our paths.
Your time does not incur worldly gain.

My Jehovah, have compassion on your children;
hear our voices.
Visit with your people; walk among us
for in your journey, you have overcome all.
I take pleasure and peace in your presence.

You Hold Me

Even though I may be broken emotionally, physically,
it is your purpose that hold me together.

Even though my spirit is laden with worries and cares,
I will cling to you.
My heart and my mind are plastered with sadness;
it is your hope that keeps me together.

Even though I am weak and sickened to walk,
pain riddling my body,
unable to stand still,
your ministry calls out my name,
beckons to me clearly.

I am committed to serving you
for here is where I am held in a solid place with you.

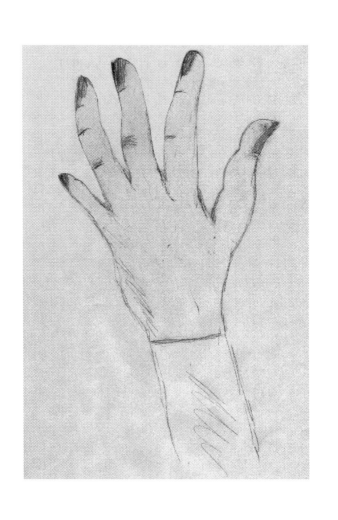

Your Portion for Me

Can I count my days as dust?
What authority do I have?
By whose instructions?

You who gave me breath;
all my days are set out clearly before you.
It is your hope that gives strength to my heart.
Therefore, I will sing before you.
You are my God, a King, a Conqueror.

All that I have acquired is your portion for me—
my family, resources, time, and health.
I smile, live, and sing because of you.
Surely you will allow me to thrive before you.

There is another who canvasses for my joy, my soul,
but these belong only for you.
Stand up, O Lord, remind me of his destiny.

Hope

Bring me, O Lord, to your dwelling place.
Show me your paths and direction.
Grant me your counsel.
Oh, my Father, grant me your work for my hands.

When my heart becomes saturated with worries and concerns,
so heavy, indeed, I stumble before you.

Questions and doubts make themselves room in my mind,
while despair looms close by.

Allow your daughter your strength.
Remind me of your victories for me,
and then I will host a parade
in your honor with your love and hope.

In Moments of Despair

———✺———

O Father,
carry me in your treasury of counsel and understanding.
When I am faced with despair
and confusion towers before me,
roll out your promises to me, O Lord.

Hew out a portion of my heart;
fill it with your understanding.
Fill me with your Holy Spirit,
and seal my heart with your strength,
so in times of drought and intense sorrows,
you may open that cavity filled with your counsel.

For it is unsealed only in times of droughts
of despair and sorrow.
Then may your daughter shine with your glories.
May she feast on your strength
during moments of calamities and deep despair.

Your Showers upon Me

O Lord, my God,
doubts and fears beckon to me.
They call after me and seek me out.

But you will bring me in your treasuries
that you lay up for me, your storehouse of hope.
Bring me to the pinnacle of your victory.

O Lord, shower me with mercy.
Be hasty to spare me.
Drown out my capacity to hoard doubts in you.

Hold me, O Lord,
for I am desolate and needy.
Bring out your reservoirs of mercies.
Let them flow where drought desires.

O Lord, spare me.
Keep me in your safe cave.
Then will I proceed when all is safe.

But what of the thunders of doubt,
the winds of fears, the rains of sadness?
They are all gone!
"They are all gone," the Lord declares.
You held me in your safe place.

Questions

—~~~—

O Lord, what has become
of the smiles of peace on my lips?
My smiles are withheld.
My joys, they recede to the shores
over the other side, far away.

Hold me in a safe zone, my God,
a place such as your rock.
Anchor me in your dwelling.
Hold me still that I may not move.

Your strength is near me.
I fathom it through my doubts.
I feel your strength through my pains.

O Lord, you are close to rescuing me.
You are so strong.
Your hands are right there, waiting.

Oh, my Father,
I have been set free from tribulations that seek me.
I am liberated in your strength;
I am delivered through your blood.

O Father, such power!
You wield such power.

You Who Reigns

I have raised my voice with doubts;
you remind me of your blood.
I raised my voice with worries;
you remind me of your victory.
I raised my voice with fears and hopelessness;
you remind me of Jesus.

What more can I show?
How much more do I have to prove my love?
Have I not spilled my blood on the cross?
Have I not silenced the evil one
that he may know his place?

"I have summoned the worlds.
I called everything into being.
I am in the storms and the howling winds.
I am a mighty fortress to reckon with.

"Where then is your voice before me?
Where lies your doubts, fears, and failures?
I have conquered them all!

"I am the great I Am," declares the Lord.

Your Deliverance for Me

—ᴖᴖ—

You lead me at all times
that I may not be enticed with dazzling, glittering stones,
stones covered in distractions from you, O Lord,
distractions laden with this world's treasures.

These are not my enemies
but are mere distractions from you.

My enemies are cunning, beautiful, and crafty.
He and his helpers draw me away from you;
his intentions lead to hopelessness for me.

My enemy has a clear path for me.
He has carefully mapped and secured his plans.

Every plan is carefully thought through,
designed only to steal, lie, and destroy.

But you, O Lord, will deliver me.
You will open my eyes to see you.
You will sustain and strengthen me.
And as for me,
I will maintain my paths before you in victory.

Clear Paths

Oh, my Father,
visit with your daughter even today.
In my home, my room, my space,
stop by where I am.

Reveal your paths before me
that I may not be scattered from you, desolate.
My journey is with you, O God,
my path, my walk.

You started, you will surely fulfill my purposes in you.
I put my hope, my trust, and my faith in you, O Lord.
Surely you will reveal the way for me to walk.

You Are in All Things

What can I say to you, O Lord?
For all things are known to you.

You discern my paths.
You know my limitations.
You see who I am and who I can become.

What then can I say before you?
"Have mercy on me, O Lord
for I am desolate before you.
I am like the thirsty traveler in the desert,
desperate for you".

I seek your counsel, your guidance.
All day long, I wait.
But you, O Lord, you are right here with me.

You hear my cries, my woes.
You long for me to see you
for you are everywhere; you are in all things.

But you will help me to focus my eyes,
my heart, my mind on you.
You will reveal yourself for you are everywhere.

You will answer me
for in your Word lie all the answers I seek.

I Write for You

My kind Jehovah, it is when I write for you
I am closest to you.
I feel lost in gratitude before you.

When I write, O Lord, my heart pours out.
My emotions, my love, my dedication
spilled out just for you.
When I write for you, O Lord,
I am in a different place; I am close to you.
I can see and feel your love for me;
it brings tears to my eyes.

You see who I really am before you.
It becomes pitiful;
I am pitiful before you.
You see who I am, yet you love me.

Have mercy on me, O Lord,
for I am known to you.

Your love and compassion for me
are greater; they far outweigh the
magnitude of your oceans
and majestic hills you created.

My Doubts

How many times have I doubted you,
O Lord of the heavens?
Is there a sum to all of it?
It is like a stumbling block in our journey.

I am limited, O God,
my thoughts, intentions limited.
You are the God of heaven and earth.
You are the God of the entire universe.
You are my God and my Jehovah.

How much pity for me,
a mortal before you,
that I should harbor doubts, doubts about you?
Yet I do.

How patient you are with your love,
gentle in your understandings.

What marvelous love!
Poured out to me, it seeps through my dry soul,
a balm for my sore heart.
Surely my feet will find themselves at your feet.